The Love of Horses

The Love of
Horses

ANNE ALCOCK

OCTOPUS BOOKS

Contents

First published 1973 *by*
Octopus Books Limited
*59 Grosvenor Street, London W*1

ISBN 0 7064 0259 6

© 1973 *Octopus Books Limited*

Distributed in USA by
Crescent Books
a division of Crown Publishers Inc
419 Park Avenue South
New York, N.Y. 10016

Distributed in Australia by
Rigby Limited
30 North Terrace, Kent Town
Adelaide, South Australia 5067

Produced by Mandarin Publishers Limited
14 Westlands Road, Quarry Bay, Hong Kong

Printed in Hong Kong

The World of Horses

Yearlings and foals from Ireland, one of the world's most famous breeding grounds for hunters. Horses have been bred in Ireland for hundreds of years and are descended from the Connemara pony, the Irish Draught Horse and the Thoroughbred. These horses usually make brilliant jumpers and are exported all over the world for hunting, show jumping and eventing. They command very high prices. The grace and elegance of these spirited youngsters at play is always an exciting sight. They nuzzle up to each other, scratch each other behind the ear or on the wither in unison, rear up and bite playfully, toss their heads and gallop about bucking and wheeling, then come back together again rearing their heads majestically against the skyline. They will tire suddenly and become quite bored with their games, and because they are hot they will lie down and roll—preferably in a warm dusty part of the field. Or they will find a suitable tree or post to rub themselves against. The foal [*below*] has sought the more peaceful company of adults.

[*above*] There is nothing like a good scratch, especially when you are living a rough life with no one to groom you.

Two horses turned out together soon learn the advantage of 'I'll scratch your back if you scratch mine'. In the hot summer weather, too, you will often see two horses standing head to tail, flicking away the flies from each other's faces as they doze in the shade of a tree.

Horses enjoy visitors or newcomers to the field, and are easily encouraged to come to the fence or gate, especially if you have a titbit to offer. However, if you haven't, they are equally happy to use you as a scratching post, or to receive a friendly rub on the nose.

[*right*] A New Forest foal finds his feet. On a drive through the New Forest you can see groups of ponies grazing, and many have become quite tame as drivers stop and feed them. But since faster roads have been built through the area, some ponies that were attracted to the roadside by offers of sugarlumps and apples have been killed or injured by fast traffic. More fences and ditches have been built, and drivers have been discouraged from feeding the ponies, or driving too fast. The ponies are not quite so tame now, but they live in greater safety. The foal [*below*] has discovered another use for his long, gangling legs. It's quite an art to balance on three legs when one is so young.

[*left*] These ponies wintering out by a stream in Devon have been given hay to supplement their natural food because the goodness has gone out of the grass until the new growth in the spring. Ideally, hay should be put into a hay net and tied up to a tree or fence at head height, or if there are several ponies in one field the hay can be put into a rick. If it is scattered on the ground, the hay gets dirty very quickly, and quite a bit is wasted.

[*below*] A Welsh Mountain Pony with her foal in the Black Mountains. All types of native British ponies are extremely hardy as a result of being turned out on moorlands and mountains to breed.

Portugal and Spain share some breeds that are common to both countries. However, the Lusitano [*left and above*] is, like the Sorraia, indigenous to Portugal. Lusitanos were used as Cavalry mounts, and they still do light agricultural work. Sometimes, too, they are trained for the bullring. The spirited young Lusitano on the left seems full of enthusiasm, but will have to be very controlled in the bullring.

The Noric Horse [*right*] comes from Austria, and is now bred in South Germany as well. Its name comes from Noricum, which was a kingdom or state within the Roman Empire. These are medium-sized working horses with fairly short legs, suitable for pulling heavy loads.

[*above left*] A young pony recently weaned from his mother looks forward to a meal of solid food. While feeding her foal, a mare needs extra nourishment to ensure a good supply of milk. A foal usually takes interest in his mother's feed at about eight weeks, but he will not be completely weaned until he is six or seven months old. Even the feeding of adult ponies should be carefully supervised if they are kept in paddocks. Depending on the size of the paddock and quality of the grass, a pony may need extra nourishment in the form of hay. There are also certain plants poisonous to horses that should neither be growing in the field nor within reach over the fence, such as yew and deadly nightshade. Grass that is very rich can also be a danger to ponies.

[*centre left*] Two attractively coloured foals make friends on Dartmoor. Ponies left to run wild have a better natural instinct as to which plants are poisonous, and are not tempted to eat them.

[*lower left*] A pony enjoying the early summer sunshine in an English orchard. Much as he would like to stay, he will be moved out when the apples grow as he cannot resist eating them in spite of the inevitable consequences – very painful colic.

In an era when many traditional country crafts are dying out, one which we cannot afford to lose is that of the blacksmith [*right*]. In many parts of Britain the shortage of farriers has reached crisis point. Blacksmiths blame the shortage on the period after the Second World War when working horses were replaced by machines and the present upsurge in riding for pleasure could scarcely be foreseen. Then younger men saw no future in the trade. Now there are lads willing to become apprentices, but a vicious circle has arisen because existing blacksmiths want ready-trained help. It takes twelve months before an apprentice can nail a shoe onto a horse, and farriers are shy of taking a young man on only to lose him later.

Fifty years ago every village had one or two forges. Nowadays, one can travel up to sixty miles to have a horse or pony shod, although riding is becoming increasingly popular.

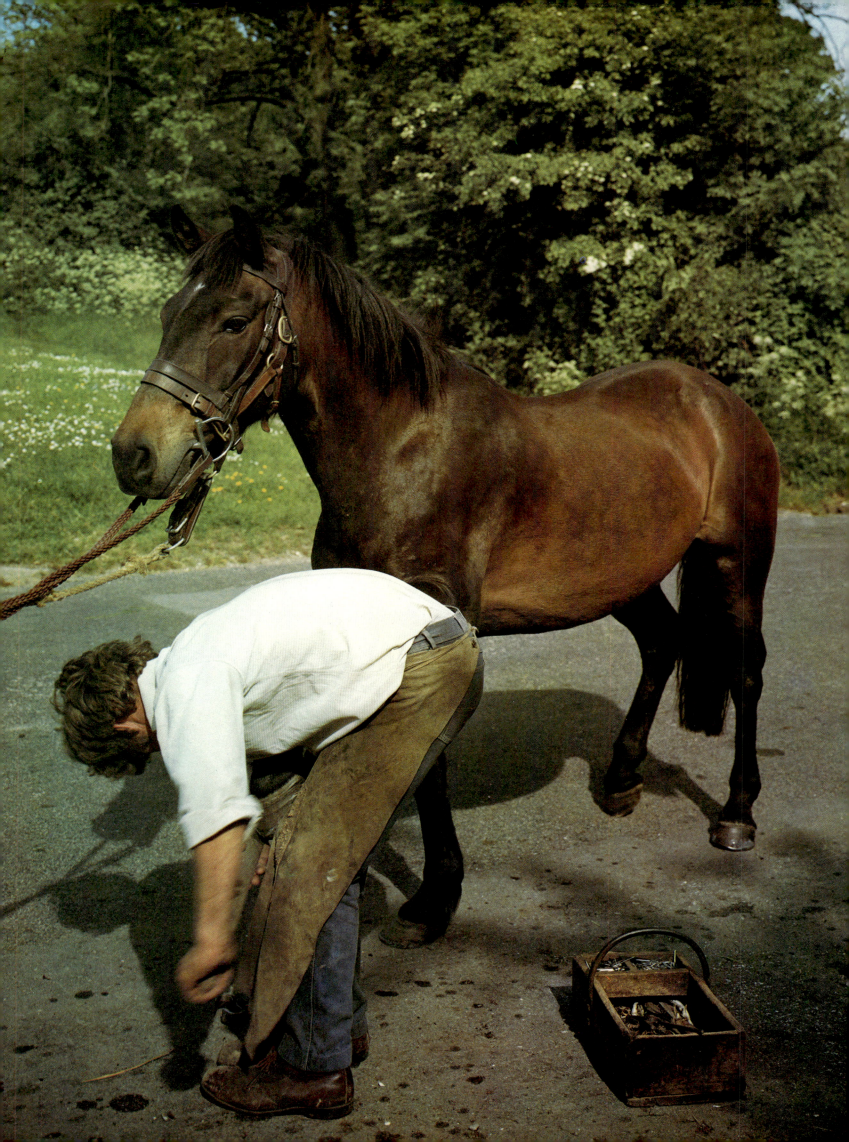

The donkey or ass plays an important part in many Eastern countries, and the picture above shows a stud ass in Morocco. He has every right to look contented, as he has an easy life compared to most of his fellow asses and donkeys who work hard carrying heavy loads, often quite long distances.

The humble donkey has come up in the world in recent years. Enthusiasts now breed him carefully, and serious faces are seen around a donkey class at a show. A casual spectator who smiles to see his woolly friends clipped out and plaited will be looked at askance. A well-bred yearling colt can fetch a considerable sum of money and breeders now specialize in producing skewbald donkeys as these are very popular. However, on the peat bog moors of Ireland a donkey is still very much a donkey. There he is a hard worker, pulling the milk cart to the dairy, carrying heavy packloads, hauling in the peat and taking the farmer to church on a Sunday. At the end of the day he is turned out on the moor [*left*], his feet sometimes hobbled to prevent him wandering too far. A driver will often turn a corner and find himself confronted by a donkey either standing in the road or lying on the warm surface. Although proverbially stubborn the donkey is more often docile and gentle.

[16]

Perhaps the most endearing of all ponies is the Shetland seen on this page, immortalized by the British cartoonist, Thelwell. The Shetland comes from very ancient stock and is a native of Northern Scotland and the islands of Orkney and Shetland. They are extremely hardy animals due to the fierce weather conditions and barren landscape of their native islands. In Great Britain the Stud Book limits their height to between twenty-six and forty-two inches, and because of this and also their even temper, they make excellent ponies for small children. In the past they were used exclusively for draught work in the coal mines of Northern England. Before rushing off at Christmas to buy that adorable pony for the children, parents should realize that once they have paid for him, their troubles are only just beginning. Their appealing new pet needs a suitable field to graze and romp in, a hut for shelter, a daily feed of hay and drink of water. When the weather is very cold, the ice has to be broken on his water trough daily. His feet must be kept well shod and he must be checked over carefully every day for cuts or sores. If parents can afford the money and the time needed to give a pony a good home, he in return will give their children years of pleasure as he teaches them the rudiments and fun of riding and looking after an animal.

Most countries have at least one indigenous breed of horse. The group in the shade of the tree on the left are Welsh Mountain Ponies, whilst the pretty face on the right belongs to the Sorraia from Portugal. Both breeds possess great hardiness and stamina as a result of generations of ancestors having lived in the wild. Welsh ponies are very agile and surefooted as they were bred to live in rough steep areas. This, along with their gentle nature, makes them very popular as children's ponies. They are also very attractive in appearance, due to infusions of Arab blood in past years. This gives the Welsh Mountain Pony a slightly dish-faced look, like the Arab. There are other types of Welsh ponies, such as the Welsh Cob, which is a larger animal, and the Welsh Pony, which was originally created by crossing the Cob with the Mountain Pony.

The Sorraia is a rarer horse [*above*]. It was for centuries used by cowboys in Portugal, and also for light farm work. Now, however, there are comparatively few left, although a small pure-bred herd is being kept to preserve them. Their colouring is often a very attractive palomino or grey, with a dark stripe along the spine.

[*right*] An Arabian mare and her beautiful foal on a stud at Phoenix, Arizona, USA. Set in a vast saucerlike valley around the Salt River and surrounded by mountains, the capital of Arizona has its landscape studded with cacti and date palms.

Working Horses

The Bavarian city of Munich, host of the 1972 Olympic Games, comes alive with merry-making for the annual October fair. During the day the streets are packed with parades and processions, while in the evenings the crowds flock to the beer cellars to drink, dance and sing. The horses pulling the Paulaner Thomas Brewery float steal the show in their gay blue and silver finery [*left*], while another driver prepares his charges before they join the parade [*above*]. The Shetland pony is not just an attractive child's pet, since he is considered to be exceptionally strong for his size. Several breweries keep horses not just because they look superb but also because they are cheaper on short trips than lorries. There is however a great deal of work involved in keeping these gentle-nature creatures, and the complicated harness, decorated with silver or brasses takes a long time to clean and prepare.

The British treasure colourful remnants of their past and throughout the year one of the most popular sights in London is the Life Guard, members of the Household Cavalry, mounting guard at Buckingham Palace and [*left*] at Whitehall. The tradition is older at Whitehall as it stems from the days when Charles II lived here and the Life Guards were formed from his own dashing cavaliers. With the exception of a grey for the trumpeter, the horses are always black and are bought, as three- or four-year-olds, mainly from Ireland.

[*above left*] A drum horse of the Household Cavalry Band parading in front of Buckingham Palace. By tradition the drum horses are piebald or skewbald and must be exceptionally strong to carry the enormous weight of two solid silver drums. The riders of these horses sit to the trot on ceremonial occasions to prevent a ragged, uneven up and

down impression. The horses are beautifully trained but it would be impossible to expect them to trot in identical rhythm. The drum horses possess the most equable of natures. Not only must they remain placid at the sound of the drum so close to their ears and unruffled amidst much bustle, but they must learn to take directions from the riders' feet which guide the reins attached to the stirrup irons, leaving the drummers' hands free to drum.

Perhaps the most elegant of all ceremonial horses are the magnificent Arab horses of the Moroccan Garde Royale, parading [*above*] in the grounds of the King's palace at Rabat. The Garde Royale is the *corps d'élite* of the Moroccan army. Their job is to act as the King's personal guard and they escort him on his weekly Friday visits to the Mosque. The stallions are stabled in sumptuous surroundings at the Royal stud at Tamara.

Beautiful Arab horses in a procession in Cairo [*above*]. The Arab is the purest and finest horse in the world. It is no wonder that the Arabs have reproduced him fanatically in the desert for at least 5,000 years as he has remarkable qualities. He has the best stamina of any known horse arising from his desert life, a beautiful presence and a free, gay movement at any pace. He is particularly clear-winded and has tendons like iron. The Arabs called their horse Kehilan, which is Arabic for thoroughbred, and it is from the Arab that the thoroughbred originated. Every thoroughbred in the world possesses some Arabian blood, and even now some thoroughbreds are born with unmistakable Arab characteristics: small, neat ears, large eyes, the dished face and wide nostrils, and the high tail carriage.

The Arab is small compared to the thoroughbred and many other native breeds of Europe, but can carry a fully grown man without trouble. They are bred in Europe, England and America, and their breeders say their horses are as pure bred as those of the Royal Jordanian stud.

Founded in 1814 by Napoleon from the élite of the French fighting forces, the *Cadre Noir* [*left*] has become one of the leading schools in Europe. It paid its first visit to England since before the 1939–45 war in October, 1972, when it received a great welcome at Wembley during the new Courvoisier Championships, performing displays each evening. The *Cadre Noir* is part of the Cavalry School at Saumur, and the selected group of horsemen practise High School riding in accordance with the classical French tradition. Although much younger than the celebrated

[24]

Spanish Riding School of Vienna, and less dedicated than those famous performers because of its involvement in two world wars and the calls of military and civilian duties, the *Cadre Noir* has nevertheless a very high standard. The agile and sturdy little Norman horses are not bred especially for the job as are the Lipizzaners of Vienna but they move with elegance and freedom. Their light and gay performances, particularly the Pas Seul, are a delight to watch. With their riders dressed in purple and gold, and their movements well designed and accurately performed, they give a magnificent display.

The coaching marathon at leading shows today [*above*] is another popular feature. It was first introduced to the Royal International Horse Show in 1909. It is judged not on speed, but on marks for the horses; their turn-out and their condition when returning to the arena from the marathon. There is a time limit for the journey and the coachman is not allowed to change.

As honest an accomplice as any policeman could wish for, the British police horse [*right*] carries out invaluable work in large cities patrolling and controlling crowds and traffic. Police horses can be seen out exercising in groups on the road early in the morning when they are not required for work that day. During the summer the police horse events are popular at large shows, and their practical tests amuse the spectators. First each horse performs a dressage test to show off his obedience and suppleness. Then he is put through an obstacle course, designed to represent the various

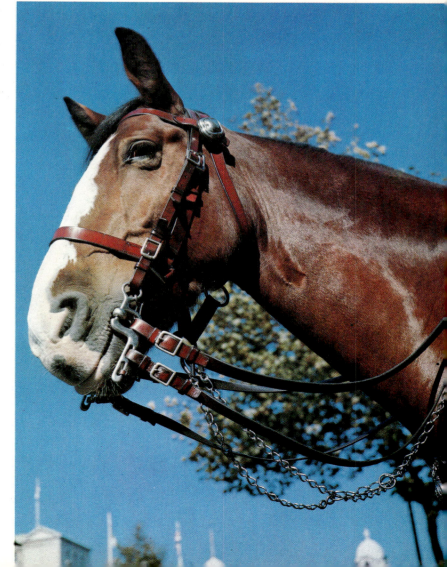

hazards he may meet with in the course of duty. His rider stops to talk to a man who then fires a pistol right beside him; he has to walk under an arch-way and as he approaches it the awning starts flapping, and he has to ride straight into a jeering mob demonstrating with waving banners and football rattles. So well trained are they that they can go through it all without turning a hair.

The work horse is a necessary part of rural life in many parts of the world but in Britain the sight of horses ploughing a field is a rare one. The heavy horses, that is the Shire, Clydesdale, Percheron and Suffolk, can pull a weight of five tons when in harness and are still used in deep mud, on steep hills where a tractor cannot climb, or for jobs where a tractor would be too big and cumbersome. However these horses are mainly seen now at country ploughing matches and the larger horse shows. These shows often include classes for mares and foals to encourage heavy horse breeding, and do much to ensure that magnificent sights like these do not disappear.

Heavy horse breeds. Left is a Shire Horse, perhaps the oldest and noblest of the heavy horses and probably a descendant of the Medieval Great Horse, a breed which was developed for military purposes. These horses have enormous strength and a pair of geldings can move weights of up to eighteen and a half tons. They are also good movers and have an elegant carriage with long legs and necks compared to the Suffolk Punch [*below left*]. Always chestnut in colour, these massive horses have a reputation for being docile and kind. The breed originated in Suffolk at about the turn of the fifteenth century, but almost every Suffolk Punch born now traces back in direct descent to a horse born in 1760. Not only are they hard working and big weight carriers but the Suffolks are renowned for longevity, and are often still at work in their twenties.

Part of the attraction of heavy horses at shows is the beautiful way they are turned out, with plumes and brasses and coloured ribbons plaited into their manes and tails. The Percheron [*top right*] has spread to many parts of the world since it was bred by farmers in the Perche district of France about 150 years ago. During the 1914–18 war thousands were purchased by Canada, Argentine and America, for despite his size, the Percheron is very active, has a kind nature and is known as the most economical of the heavy breeds. They proved most successful at hauling guns and willingly trotted on the hard, rough roads day after day between the troops.

The Clydesdale [*centre*] is extremely popular both in its native Scotland and abroad and an increasing number are exported to America, the Commonwealth and other foreign countries every year. They have been bred over the centuries to have particularly strong and well-formed legs and feet and are known for their high, clean, action.
A Breton horse [*right*] at stud at Lamballe, Brittany, bearing the Breton brand. The stud is part of the French National Stud which has centres for different breeds all over the country. Like so many heavy horses the Breton is known for its docility. It is bred in three different sizes, the heavy draught, draught post and mountain draught. It is one of the smaller heavyweight breeds, is popular for agricultural work, and has been sold to many countries, especially Italy and Spain.

[29]

Another pony bred for work is the Fjord pony of Norway [*above*]. The common feature of this animal is his dun colouring with the black dorsal stripe. A certain amount of Arab blood in him has made him more distinguished than many working breeds nowadays, but his ancestors have been known in Scandinavia for centuries.

It takes a strong animal to pull a sledge loaded with rocks, and with his head down, and his mouth open this Finnish draught horse at Tpaja is using the full strength of his muscles to master the load [*below*]. The large majority of the some 180,000 horses in Finland are of the draught type and their work on the farms and, more especially, in the forests, is invaluable. Finland is another country where the stallions and mares of the particular breeds pass stringent tests before being accepted in the stud book.

The abundance of native European ponies which have lived

for centuries in a wild state means that there is a large supply of hardy animals all useful for working purposes. The four breeds on these two pages all demonstrate this point admirably. Haflinger ponies, like the two pictured above, have the national flower of Austria, the edelweiss, with an H in the middle, as their brand. They are usually palomino or chestnut with flaxen manes and tails and this attractive and appealing colouring, combined with their great capacity for hard work and ability to exist in any conditions has gained them great popularity throughtout the world.

The Noric Horse [*below*] is of mixed European origin and, as with other Continental breeds, is not allowed to become a stud book stallion until it has shown its ability and willingness in harness. It must also pull a load of a certain weight, and walk and trot measured distances in a given time.

The work of the North American cutting pony is very skilled and demands great intelligence, speed and agility on the part of both pony and rider. A cutting pony inherits the instinct for the work as a sheepdog does for rounding up sheep, and yet the unity of purpose between rider and pony, the instant obedience of the animal to the man and the skill of both still amaze anyone who watches them at work. His intelligence is evident and he obviously enjoys every minute. He senses the moment his rider has selected a particular steer, and he will not rest until the beast is cut out from the rest.

The popular rodeo shows arose out of the everyday work of the cowboys, though it is easy to forget that there is more to a rodeo show than staying aboard a bucking bronco. There are usually classes to test the competitors' skill in cuttingout calves, driving wagons and bull-dogging, all sports which are based on the skills needed back at the ranch [*above*]. The horse has stalled as soon as the calf has been successfully roped, thus acting like an anchor and assisting the cowboy with his task of securing the calf. Probably the greatest rodeo show is the Calgary Stampede in Alberta, Canada. An annual week-long feast of merry-making, it encourages the finest cowboys to pit their wits against each other and the animals. Visitors from all parts of the world enjoy coca-cola, hot dogs and doughnuts and join the throng watching races between wagons pulled by four horses apiece, musical chairs on horse-back, wild cow milking contests, and all the various rodeo events. The gaiety is infectious and the bars remain open most of the night.

Stockmen leaving their ranch to round up cattle; a long, hard task for a horse and his rider. Most stock horses are of Arab blood and so able to carry a man and heavy stock saddle complete with rope and other necessities all day.

Show Jumping & Eventing

In the picture on the left a crowd watches a puissance competition in the USA. This type of high-jump test is a bone of contention among horse-lovers, as some people say it pushes a horse beyond its capabilities until it is forced to fault. A puissance competition has about six fences in the first round, at a height of up to five feet three inches. Those who have a clear round jump off over fewer but higher fences, until the final horses are left with two fences to attempt. The indoor jumping record is seven feet three inches and was achieved by Raymond Howe on the Australian-bred *Kalkallo Prince* at the Horse of the Year Show, Wembley in 1972. An upright fence such as the one on the left is even harder for a horse as there is no ground line to help him to know where to take off. The British outdoor high-jump record has remained at seven feet six and a quarter inches, jumped by Donald Beard on *Swank* at the 1938 Olympic Games.

[*right*] An unusual view of leading National Hunt jockey Terry Biddle-combe. The occasion is the jockeys' show-jumping competition at the Horse of the Year Show, Wembley. It is a popular and colourful event and makes a bright interlude for the spectators from the usual classes. The jockeys all wear racing colours and many of them are lent suitable horses. The most striking feature of the event is the jockeys' style; some of them keep their stirrup leathers short, some slip their reins and sit back as they would over a fixed fence, and many of them ride much faster than most show-jumpers.

[*following page left*] Bill Steinkraus competing in the 1971 Nations Cup at Hickstead. Steinkraus has been called the doyen of American show jumpers. He is captain of the American team and has been taking part in the four-yearly Olympic Games since 1952. He is a perfectionist oand maintains a remarkable

record whatever horse he is riding. Unlike most riders, he is not identified with one particular horse. He is seen here on *Fleet Apple*, typical of American hunters who seem to tackle the highest fences with effortless ease.

Harvey Smith, the dour Yorkshireman who has captured the hearts of show-jumping spectators, seen [*below left*] on *Johnny Walker* at the All-England Jumping Course at Hickstead. As a horsemaster he has few rivals, and as a man with a sense of humour he is much loved. He has the grim-faced determination that this tough sport needs now, though he announced in 1972 that he was planning to turn professional in which case he will not represent Britain for a third time in the next Olympic Games.

Ann Moore [*top right*] is one of the ablest and most attractive of the women show-jumpers. She has won major competitions in many different countries, and narrowly missed the individual show-jumping gold medal in the 1972 Munich Olympic Games. She is a former Junior European show-jumper, and currently holds the adult European Ladies title. She has caught the imagination of the general public with *Psalm* almost as much as did Marion Mould (*née* Coakes) on her phenomenal pony, *Stroller*. Here, Ann is taking *Psalm* down the famous ten feet six inch Hickstead Derby bank during the 1970 jumping Derby. The bank is used only once a year, and after twelve years of controversy over its safety, it claimed, sadly, a victim in 1972 and is now to be modified. In its history, the jumping Derby has brought just twelve clear rounds, three of them from *Stroller*.

Local shows play an important part in the rise to fame of show-jumping stars. This young girl [*right*] has got her pony beautifully balanced and she is looking ahead to the next fence, anticipating how best to take her mount up to it. At shows like this the child with the most ordinary pony competes on equal terms with the child whose parents have bought her an expensive, well-bred one. But the most important point is the child's own love of jumping, determination and competitive spirit, and in her rise to the top she will learn more from riding difficult ponies than she will from that expensive and well-mannered mount.

[37]

Dressage is founded on a horse's basic training, and is in itself the foundation of specific equine training such as racing, or advanced dressage, performed in the Olympic Games. The horse that is good at dressage is supple, smooth and obedient to the rider's aids. Many top show-jumpers, particularly Germans, will perform a little dressage when they enter the show-jumping ring. The high-class movements of the Spanish Riding School and *Cadre Noir* cannot be taught until the horse has learnt basic dressage.

[*above left*] Jennie Loriston-Clarke, sister of Michael and Jane Bullen, riding her horse, *Kadett*, in the 1972 Munich Olympic Games. It was the fourth consecutive Olympiad in which a member of the family had represented Britain. Michael rode in the three-day event at Rome in 1960 and at Tokyo in 1964, and Jane rode *Our Nobby* to a team gold medal in Mexico in 1968. Equestrian events have been included in the modern Olympics since 1912.

[*below left*] Upright but relaxed, Richard Meade enters the arena on *The Poacher*, perfectly poised for the task ahead. Meade, at thirty-four years old, is one of the most experienced of Britain's three-day event riders. *The Poacher* was a consistently good gelding although he never competed in the Olympic Games. Meade finished eighth in the Tokyo Olympics riding *Barbery*, was a member of the gold medal team in Mexico where he roade *Cornishman V*, and then in the 1972 Olympics he rode *Laurieston* to both individual and team victories.

Many local horse shows will include a dressage event in their programme, but it is fairly unusual to see a participant riding sidesaddle, like the lady on the right.

[above] A close-up study of the 1971 European horse trials champion, HRH Princess Anne. Here she is on *Doublet* landing over a fence on the steeplechase phase of the Crookham horse trials, demonstrating a perfect seat and steady pair of hands. *Doublet* was a home-bred horse by *Doubtless* out of a polo pony, and Princess Anne developed a wonderful partnership with him. After their sudden and well-earned success at Burghley in 1971 it was particularly disappointing that *Doublet* was unsound during most of 1972.

[below] The scene is taking place in Britain, the flag is American, and the horse and rider Australian. Brian Schrapel takes *Wakool* over a fence in the show-jumping phase of the Tidworth horse trials.

[above right] A really nasty-looking fall, and this is what makes eventing a sport for the brave. In racing, which is quite nerve-racking enough, the horses are ridden in hot blood and there is a certain amount of give in the fences. In eventing, horse and rider go off alone in cold blood to tackle fences which, if not cleared, will produce this sort of result. The big difference between the two is in speed, and where the event rider can check, and persuade his horse to measure the fence correctly, every jump jockey knows the feeling only too well of going into a fence at full gallop when everything might go wrong. Breasting the Z rails on the

Crookham cross-country course is *Minivet* ridden by Mr Richard Vines.

[*below*] Mary Gordon-Watson and *Cornishman V* – World Champions, European Champions, and Olympic Gold Medallists. They make a very attractive combination at the top of the three-day eventing tree. Mary, from Dorset in England, is surprisingly slight with a charming smile and winning personality, and has borne the inevitable disappointments of the sport as bravely as she has taken successes modestly. Few horses have been so consistent in the topsy-turvy world of eventing than the great, handsome thoroughbred *Cornishman V*. He was first ridden to an Olympic gold medal by Richard Meade in Mexico, leaving Mary in the unenviable position of trying to live up to his triumph. She quickly dispelled any doubts that she was not up to the task. Here she is taking the water on the way to a team gold medal in the Munich Olympics, and fourth overall position. She is leaning back to be properly balanced for the downhill jump (if she leant forward she might be catapulted into the water) and she has slipped the reins to prevent interference with the horse's mouth. *Cornishman V* is one of the great personalities of the horse world, and his intelligent face and sharply pricked ears appearing over the top of a cross-country fence are instantly recognizable.

Course builders love to include a water obstacle on a cross-country course. It provides a spectacle and invariably bears some influence on the final result. A horse needs to have complete trust in his rider to jump unhesitatingly into water. Even in drought-ridden Australia a course builder has included a water splash [above].

The one thing that emerges clearly through the spray on the left is that the competitor is an American. In fact it is Bruce Davidson on the appropriately named *Plain Sailing*, in the Munich Olympic Games. They put in one of the best cross-country performances of the Games.

[below] Mrs M. F. Jones and the equally appropriately named *Farewell*, part company at the seventeenth jump in the Badminton Horse Trials. Britain's premier three-day event is set in the lovely Gloucestershire park of the Duke of Beaufort, and to ride there is the ambition of many up-and-coming riders. The four and a half mile gruelling cross-country course demands the greatest courage from horses and riders, and all in all these competitions provide the world's most thorough and comprehensive equine tests. A high-class horse with courage and speed is required for the cross-country phase, but that same horse must be settled and calm enough to perform the testing dressage test obediently on the first day. On the second day some twenty miles are ridden altogether. First comes a hack along roads and tracks, mainly taken at the trot or walk. Then there is a two and a half mile steeplechase course, followed by more roads and tracks and finally the cross-country section, which exerts the biggest influence on the end result of the event. The show-jumping on the third day is held to demonstrate that the horse is still sound and supple and can jump, not necessarily very high or far, but accurately and at the speed required.

European Horses & Ponies

The Arab [*left*], showing off his ancient facial features, the dish face, neat ears, wide dark eyes, flared nostrils – the equine epitomy of elegance and beauty. This is the oldest and purest breed in the world. Drawings and carvings of Arabs have been found dating back to many centuries BC, and there are records of named horses of 5,000 years ago. Their existence has been guarded so fanatically by breeders that their ancient qualities have in no way diminished. They can still survive in the desert and endure long journeys.

[*above*] Arabian mares and foals gather together under an ancient wall. Arab horses were brought west with a series of Islamic invasions. This meant that breeds which were native to various European countries absorbed a certain amount of Arab blood, which in many cases enhanced the characteristics of the original breeds. Arabs are bred as enthusiastically in Europe as they are in their native lands, although they have a tendency to be larger and are different in character to those in the East.

[*above*] A tightly bunched group of
mares and foals at Kiskunsag, Hungary,
a country that is proud of its interest in
horses. Indeed, 900 years ago its horses
were so popular in Europe that their
export was banned by the king of
Hungary, for fear of over-diminishing
the home stock. In the successive
centuries breeding has been encouraged,
and the British thoroughbred has
played an important part in this. Large
studs were established (there were 4,000
mares at one stud in 1810), with many
thoroughbreds and Arab stallions, and in
1876 the winner of the Derby came
from Kisber. The Shagya Arab was
developed from a desert Arab strain,
and the modern horses are excellent
movers and possess most of the qualities
of the pure Arab. The Hungarians are
also very keen on trotting races. The
three best known Hungarian breeds are
the Furioso (from an English foundation
stallion who sired ninety-five stallions),
the Murakosi, developed in the last fifty
years with a heavy Percheron and
Ardennes influence on native mares, and
the Nonius, founded from a French/
English horse that was captured by the
Hungarian cavalry during the
Napoleonic wars.
About ten years ago a Danishman called

Nyegaard fell in love with the Hungarian Shagya Arab. He went to Hungary and bought some of the best Shagyas that could be found. He brought them all home to Barthahus near Copenhagen and employed a Hungarian studman to look after them. The Barthahus Stud is now well established and a riding school is run successfully in conjunction with it. The mare and foal in a field with the rest of the herd [*below left*], and the horses playing follow-my-leader in the photograph [*above right*] are all Shagya Arabs at Nyegaard's stud at Barthahus. They obviously appreciate the fertile surroundings in Denmark in which they are now living.

The Hungarian Furioso [*right*] derives its name from the founder stallion, who was imported from England in about 1840, and it is now a well-known half-bred strain. Furioso quickly bred ninety-five stallions which were distributed throughout the old Austrian empire. The breed can now be found in Czechoslovakia, Poland, and Rumania as well as Hungary and Austria. They make good looking, active, saddle horses and shine in trotting competitions and local races.

The Friesian horse of the Netherlands [*left*], which is always black, dates back some 3,000 years, and its ancestors are said to have survived the Ice Age. This was the most popular horse in the Middle Ages, and was used to carry heavy armoured knights into battle and for work on the land. Crusading knights brought home eastern stallions which increased the Friesians' qualities and when trotting became a popular national pastime, the breed was lightened further. Through this the breed lost favour as a general purpose horse and was actually in danger of dying out. In 1913 only three stallions were left. Luckily a new breed society was formed, and gradually the numbers were built up and the Friesians regained popularity. Breeding is now controlled, and to obtain a licence a stallion must undergo a thorough veterinary test. It has become a tradition in Holland for Friesians to draw gigs in the show ring with the occupants wearing the attractive Friesian costume, often parading to the tune of the Friesian national anthem.

Appaloosas are not the only horses to have spots. On the right is the Danish Knabstrup, which was bred from one foundation mare, whose son became the foundation stallion. The breed owes its existence first to chance, and secondly to a Danish family dedicated to producing a good riding horse. The first mare, called *Flaebehoppen*, was left behind by a Spanish officer stationed in Denmark during the Napoleonic wars. She was put to work pulling a butcher's cart and, in this humble role, proved herself to be of outstanding stamina and speed. She was then bought by a Major Villars Lunn, owner of the Knabstrub estate, who, like his father before him, laid special stress on breeding riding horses with hardiness, speed and endurance. In 1812 she was put to a palomino stallion and produced the spotted colt *Flaebehingsten*. In its comparatively short history the breed has thrived and many of the horses find their way to circuses.

Another type of spotted horse is seen [*left*]: the Pinzgauer from Austria. This used to be a breed in its own right but now it is considered as a sub-variety of the Austrian Noric Horse.

The grey Lipizzaners are famed as the horses of the Spanish Riding School of Vienna. Other colours are bred but are not used for the school. The breed is now four centuries old, and its fine presence, bold head and intelligent temperament has made it outstanding as a carriage, ceremonial and riding horse. Despite the name of the riding school, the Airs they perform there are not Spanish. They originate from the English Duke of Newcastle and the Frenchman, Antonius de Pluvinal, who was riding instructor to Louis XIII. The horses in the picture [*below*] were bred in Hungary, one of the chief breeding grounds of the Lipizzaner.

The Spanish Riding School of Vienna probably produces the best-trained horses and the finest horsemen in the world. Since the late sixteenth century the art of horsemanship has been practised here in its highest form until today it must be the nearest thing to perfection in horse riding. Tremendous patience and dedication is shown in training the magnificent Lipizzaner stallions and even the riders serve ten to fifteen years' apprenticeship before finishing as a *Bereiter,* that is, fully qualified to train a stallion. Although the Lipizzaners have been an Austrian breed since 1580 they were derived from a cross between a Spanish horse and a small Italian horse, with a later addition of Arab blood. Archduke Charles, son of the Emperor Ferdinand I, founded the Lipizzaners on his Lipizzer Stud Farm. Their adult home since 1735 has been the magnificent Spanish Riding School, built by Emperor Charles VI. Born black, the riding school horses turn grey when mature and the particular mixture in their breeding produces elegance, grace and dignity combined with strength and good looks.

One of the features of the display is the *pesade,* illustrated here [*left*]. Many of the items in the Spanish Riding School and *Cadre Noir* displays are taken directly from the cavalry exercises performed during medieval battles to frighten the enemy infantry.

[*above right*] A group of Haflinger ponies high up in the Dolomites. This breed is also native to Austria, and it is common to raise young stock on the alpine pastures so that their hearts and lungs can develop to the maximum.

The North Swedish Horse is typical of the Scandinavian breeds. The mare in the top left-hand picture is sturdy and strong, and the foal well-developed. Despite their thick bodies these horses are agile and nimble-footed. They cope admirably with the cold climate and work hard pulling timber carts or sleighs. The breed has been improved in the last fifty years by the government's strict policy that a horse must be passed by a vet, and its strength tested by pulling logs along a rough road before it can be used as a stallion. Then, when the offspring are mature, both mares and stallions are subjected to a similar test, and their legs and hooves examined. Half the timber cut in Sweden is hauled by horses, and the government has made their welfare its concern. The horses work hard at a job ranking high in the country's importance, as about one third of Sweden's exports is timber.

The racehorse in miniature [*left*]. The English thoroughbred is the fastest sprint horse in the world. Already the qualities can be seen in this foal, with long, sloping shoulders, good quarters and refined head. His ribs are well-sprung giving a barrel shape, and there is ample heart and lung room. No other breed can seriously challenge him as a racehorse and he stands supreme, together with the Arab, at the pinnacle of the equine world.

The Cleveland Bay [*above right*] is another old British breed that is extremely popular in cross-breeding. Cleveland Bays have a natural talent for jumping, and they are often crossed with thoroughbreds to produce excellent hunters and show-jumpers.

When it was time for my Welsh Mountain to be turned in for a bigger horse it was a little disappointing to be

given an old gentleman's cob like the one [*right*]. His old-fashioned, short-backed, stocky frame was hardly the teenager's ideal of a classy eventer but, realizing I was lucky to have anything, I made the most of it. Over the years that cob became a hunter who always finished a run up with hounds, who learnt enough about spreading over a show jump to be fun, and who, through sheer constancy, managed to win more than one hundred trials, beating thoroughbreds! In between times he was used as a lead horse when schooling young racehorses over hurdles; he also did well in the show-ring, and he became a real family horse, patient and affectionate with young and old, novice or experienced rider alike. His versatility and character made him very endearing. And in the end it was in the more accustomed role of gentleman's cob that he found himself; carrying the weight of a big man over any obstacle out hunting, and displaying perfect manners when hacking home. His short back, big, round quarters, high tail, stocky legs, deep girth and hogged mane carried a fine, intelligent head, and we loved him.

[*above right*] The Portuguese bullfighting horse in all his regalia. This short-backed, power-packed horse is very nimble and moves so adroitly that he is seldom hit. He is not even padded, and in fact the bull is also rarely hurt. A good horse becomes a valuable and prized possession, and is not regarded as 'bull fodder' for the entertainment of the crowds. The horses are trained for years, and many never reach the arena. Those that do must be prepared to charge head-on at the bull, only darting away at the last possible moment. The horse [*lower right*] is practising against a non-fighting heifer to gain confidence. The best fighting bulls are not destined for slaughter but are saved for breeding. Nowadays when the bull has been subdued by the skill and perseverance of horse and rider it is led away, although this has not always been the case. Bullfighting began several hundred years BC, and became popular under Julius Caesar. It was turned into a mounted sport under Tiberius Claudius and then became established in Spain, Portugal, and later on in Latin America.

Very different from the Portuguese horses, yet used for herding cattle, are the Camargue ponies, who live in semi-wild herds in the marshy area of the Rhône delta in France. The Camargue ponies, along with other wildlife there, are jealously preserved so they can lead a natural life. These all-white ponies have been trained for bullfighting in Provence, and they are sometimes rounded up by local farmers for branding. They are usually counted and turned away again, but a few will be broken in for farm work. It is thought that they are one of the oldest breeds and that they have oriental or Barb blood. The black bulls, white horses, sheep, sea-birds, flamingoes and bustards roam the 290 square miles at will. They survive hard winters and scorching summers, with the mistral blowing from the north. Only the river banks are fertile and cultivated, as much of the area is stagnant, salty marsh. Inlets in the protecting sea-dike let in water for the lagoon fisheries and saltpans, and the river water is used for irrigation and to submerge vines.

[*below left*] The mealy-muzzled Exmoor pony and his neighbour, the Dartmoor [*left*]. Both breeds are indigenous to the moors, and life is a question of the survival of the fittest. They have to face up to the elements without shelter, and with poor and scanty food. Their high action stems from constantly picking their way across rough ground, bogs and rabbit warrens. Occasionally they are rounded up for branding, and some are caught to be broken in. They are naturally hardy, and they make good, economic children's ponies, as well as being sturdy enough to carry men. The purity of the Dartmoor was endangered during the time when small ponies were needed to work in the coal mines. To try and breed a smaller pit pony, Shetland stallions were turned out on the moor, but luckily some individual breeders came to the rescue and maintained the ancient Dartmoor line.

[*right*] A splendid Connemara pony. He has been a native of this rugged region of western Ireland, from time immemorial. The legend that he originates from the horses of the Spanish Armada that were shipwrecked off-shore is certainly false and it is much more likely that he stems, along with other cold-blooded horses of northern Europe, from the wild horse of Mongolia. He probably had an addition of Spanish and Arab blood when the Galway merchants traded with Spain. Visitors can see him roaming free in his native territory much as they can other native British breeds. He makes a good child's pony as he is bigger than Dartmoor, Exmoor, and New Forest ponies.

[*right*] An Icelandic pony. The first settlers in Iceland were Norwegian refugees who moved there in the ninth century, along with their ponies. Others followed, and some brought horses from Ireland as well as Norway. Present-day Icelandic horses stem from the crosses of these, and follow the tough, cold-blooded strain of North-West Europe. The early settlers not only worked their horses hard but indulged in horsefights and, until converted to Christianity at the end of the tenth century, they ate horseflesh too. For a thousand years horses were the only form of transport in Iceland. Icelandic ponies have an unusual homing instinct and it is customary to turn them loose at the end of a long journey, when they will find their own way home in twenty-four hours.

[*left*] New Forest ponies are bigger than Dartmoors and Exmoors, but they are all similar in that they all survive on poor pasture and heathland. When bought for a child the ponies remain hardy, are economic to feed, and good in traffic. Over 2,000 ponies roam in the New Forest, with about 150 stallions. In order to maintain a good standard, the stallions are inspected each year, and inferior ones may not be kept there.

[*below left*] The hardiest of all ponies is also the smallest, the popular Shetland. Sometimes when snow is on the ground the ponies of the Shetland Isles survive on seaweed. Even when bred in warmer, southern climes, the pony's size has hardly increased. Life has become better for him in recent times as a pet. While existence as a pack pony was not hard on the sturdy character, no animal could survive many years working in the coal mines. The 'Sheltie' is a lovable, loving pony, with a thick woolly coat, small, neat head and neat short ears and he has been responsible for helping many children find confidence on horseback. His lifespan is exceptionally long, and he can compete on equal terms with large ponies and horses in obstacle driving competitions, when his compactness compensates for his lack of pace. He is so versatile that he can even keep a lawn neatly trimmed without damaging the turf, and I have even seen one brought indoors as if he were a dog!

The Fjord pony [*top left*] is Norway's invaluable native pony. Much of the heavy work that these ponies used to do has been taken over by tractors, but in fact there are certain jobs that only a pony can do, particularly on the very steep slopes of Norwegian mountains. So he remains a popular and useful friend to many Norwegian farmers.

[*top right*] This Welsh Mountain Pony has the characteristics typical of the breed and is very like my own old ply. Born in the Black Mountains of Breconshire he

[58]

roamed freely till he was two. Then he was brought to the south of England and trained as a child's pony and came to our stables. Life was always busy and he always enjoyed it to the full, with the hunting in winter, and the gymkhanas in summer. He had a phenomenal jump and he learnt to stop himself in the gymkhana games the moment the music ended, or bend in and out of poles with minimum assistance. No day out hunting was too long for him, he kept up with the rest of the field and sometimes showed the horses how to jump a tricky obstacle or negotiate a steep bank and stream. His good looks, reminiscent of the Arab, won him show-ring prizes. Now he has returned to his native Wales in semi-retirement, to teach a new generation of future riders.

The Dales pony [*right*] is a native of the border counties. These are strong, hard-working animals and at one time were used in the mines. They have been valued for hundreds of years as pack ponies and are still used on the moors, particularly in bad weather, for such jobs as taking food to isolated sheep.

Scenes from Russia

USSR has an intensive programme of horse-breeding, and has set up a system of State Studs for this purpose. There are several geographical and climatic areas within Russia and different breeds of horses have developed different characteristics to suit the various localities. Forty breeds are now recognized in Russia, and some of the native breeds have been improved by crossing with imported Thoroughbreds and Arabians. The picture on the left shows Russian Don horses pulling the Tachanka, a racing vehicle, and they certainly make a stirring sight.

The outstanding feature of the Akhal Teké breed, the Russians' desert horse [*right*], is the gleaming metallic colour of its coat when the sun shines on it. Another very unusual feature is the shortness of its mane and tail. The Akhal Teké, believed to be as old and as pure as the Arab, goes back some 2,500 years. Because the conditions of the desert are so adverse for horse breeding, it is interesting to learn how the Turkmenian people have succeeded in producing such an outstanding breed. The horses are kept permanently tied and rugged up, and are fed on foodstuffs specially produced for their high nutritious content. Not only do they survive desert conditions well, but they are also outstanding competition horses for jumping, dressage and non-thoroughbred racing.

Several thousand feet up in the Russian Caucasus the Kabardine horses are turned out all the year round. They roam in herds and each stallion has about thirty mares. They are turned loose in the mountains for most of the year and breed wild. Each stallion establishes a herd for himself, called a 'Tabun', which he guards closely and jealously. Usually Kabardines are bay and black in colour, and have an even temperament. They are comparatively short-legged, and this makes them very surefooted in the beautiful but treacherous terrain in which they are allowed to run wild. They have excellent stamina, and in fact have been proved to have greater endurance than other Russian horses.

Once a year the cossacks go up into the mountains, an expedition which may take several days, to round up the 'Tabuns' and bring the mares and foals back to the corral to be sorted out into groups [*left*]. Some will be sold, others kept for breaking and the remainder turned out again to rejoin their stallion. Right is one of the stallions which was caught especially for the photographer's visit and held for a few difficult moments. A stallion that is turned out with his mares for most of the year is virtually wild and does not take kindly to restraint of any kind. On the following page the Kabardine stallion is shown galloping back to freedom.

[63]

Below left are three Don Foals. These horses are usually chestnut. This was their original colour in the eighteenth century, but up until the beginning of this century stallions of other breeds were turned loose with the herds of mares, so that a certain amount of cross-breeding occurred. However an effort has been made in this century to keep the strain pure. Dons are tall thickset working horses, able to endure the Russian winter fending for themselves on the Steppes where they live in herds. They were the original horses of the Cossacks and are still widely used as all-purpose working horses and particularly by shepherds in the Steppe regions, and on the farms in semi-desert areas in Russia.

Another ancient Russian breed is the Karabair [*right*], believed to be some 2,400 years old. It was used in the eighteenth century to improve the Don stock. This grey is at the breed's main centre in Samarkand, one-time home of Ghengis Khan, the great Mongol Conqueror who, between 1162 and 1227, extended his empire from the Pacific to the Northern shores of the Black Sea. The very ancient Uzbekistan city contains much old Moslem architecture and this pillar is part of the buildings which surround the Registan or main square. The Karabair is another Russian breed which thrives on hard work as well as being popular for local competitions which usually consist of a few races for thoroughbreds, as well as many for other breeds.

The Lokai is a desert-type horse bred on collective and state farms in the Tadjikistan area of Russia, and is a popular mount for local racing. The rider here is wearing ceremonial Tadjik costume. The horses are used for mountain work as pack or riding horses, and are renowned for possessing such tough feet that they do not have to wear shoes for working on the rough tracks. The most usual colours are grey, bay and chestnut, and some horses have curly hair not dissimilar to Astrakhan fur. Again this breed of horse has good stamina and can work consistently well at very high altitudes.

The Malokaracheyev Stud is the most famous centre for the Kabardine breed, and below left is one of the cossacks who works permanently with the horses with his hard-working, long-suffering Kabardine. These horses are given a rigorous training so that they do not get excited when they come into contact with the semi-wild mares of the Tabun.

It is interesting to compare the gleaming Akhal-Teké stallion [*top right*] with the Moroccan Arab [*below*], which is perhaps the purest and finest horse in the world. Both horses have a similar stance and an extraordinarily alert head carriage. When visiting Russia in 1888, Sir Charles MacGregor described the Akhal-Teké as 'by far and away the best oriental horse, after Arabs, I have ever seen'. He added that they would be well suited as chargers or ladies' horses in India. There is considerable rivalry between the horse experts as to which is the oldest breed, since the Akhal-Teké is considered by its breeders to be as old if not older than the Arab. The champion Akhal-Tekés are bred in Turkmenistan, and no interbreeding is allowed.

Horses in America & Australia

The Pinto is one of America's most popular horses. However, it is not a breed, and the name 'Pinto' describes the colouring which can occur on mnay different breeds of horse and pony. There are two specific types, the piebald whose colours are black and white, and the skewbald where the colouring is white with any colour other than just black. In addition to this, Pintos are classed either as Ovaro, where a black or brown colour forms a background for white patches [above], or Tobiano where the background colour is white with coloured patches, as seen on the skewbald [left]. These horses were favoured by Indian tribes, probably because their colour served so well as camouflage. The name Pinto derives from the Spanish *pintado*, meaning painted, and refers to the Indian custom of painting designs or symbols on the white patches of their horses. The Ovaro and the grey [above], and the rest of the herd [below], live in

Virginia, where horses have roamed wild or been bred ever since the pioneering days of the seventeenth century. This part of America is one of the most popular areas for rearing horses because of the excellent grazing to be found there. As each new group of European settlers, such as the English, the Irish, the Swedes or the Dutch arrived, they would bring over their own breeds. The Quarter Horse, for example, can trace its ancestry back to these early times.
Left is a Pinto being ridden along the beach on the West coast of America. Riding in the sea is excellent therapy for a horse with weak legs and is good for all horses so that anyone close enough to the sea has a distinct advantage over the person who can only hose a horse's legs each day.
Some trainers gallop their horses on the sand but this is not always a good idea for the sand can be too hard and there are soft patches which cannot be seen until too late.

The Tennessee Walking Horse, a breed peculiar to the United States, was bred for plantation work. He had to have endurance rather than speed for he had to carry his master for miles to inspect the estates. The distinctive smooth gait was developed to give his gentleman rider as comfortable a ride as possible. Nowadays, however, this horse is bred primarily for pleasure and show, firstly because of his characteristic running walk; and secondly because of his very even temper. Indeed the breed is so popular amongst riders in America that the breed show in Tennessee is one of the most highly attended horse shows in the country. [*left*] Two Tennessee Walking Horses being put through their paces.

Just one horse gave its name to the Morgan breed [*top right*] and before he became a sire he was considered so ordinary that he was unnamed, being simply Justin Morgan's horse. It was in Massachusetts in about 1790 that the colt was given to an inn-keeper Thomas Justin Morgan in payment of a debt. He was essentially a working horse but on the side he earned his owner money from stud fees, weight-pulling contests, and racing. The phenomenal feature about this extraordinarily tough little horse was the way in which, no matter what sort of mare he mated, it was his own fine qualities and looks that were passed on. He was eventually bought by the US army who established the Morgan Stud Farm. He died in 1821 having founded America's most famous all-purpose breed.

The American Saddle-bred Horse [*centre right*] and the American Standard-bred [*below right*] are both strains that were developed for specific purposes. The Saddle Horse was bred to carry wealthy plantation owners for long hours around their estates, and to do it as comfortably as possible. Hence his movements are extremely smooth, in fact the five-gaited Saddle Horse can manage two extra artificial movements: the slow-gait, where each foot is raised and lowered separately in a prancing motion, and the rack which is a dramatic high-speed version of the slow-gait. The Standard-bred [*right*] comes from a line of trotters and thoroughbreds. They were quickly recognized as a formal breed, and now a Standard-bred that can race a mile in a standard one minute twenty seconds is accepted by the stud book.

[71]

[*left*] American round-up. Clouds of dust fly as a large herd of horses gallops down the hillside into the corral.

A group of horses grazing in the USA [*above*]. It is usual for horses to stay close to each other when they are turned out, even if there is plenty of land open to them. This instinct may be handed down from the days of wild herds when for safety's sake they had to stay close together. Among this group is an Appaloosa or spotted horse. Spotted horses were first recorded by the Chinese 3,000 years ago. More recently they were intensively bred by the Nez Perce Indians of the Palouse country in Central Idaho and Eastern Washington. This tribe was wiped out in a battle with the US army in 1877, but the breed survived and today is one of the most popular types in America particularly as a circus horse. The spots are superimposed on the silky grey coat, and can actually be felt. They are black or chocolate, although the skin of an Appaloosa is pink.

[*right*] Chincoteague ponies come from an island of the same name off the coast of Virginia and Maryland. They are usually piebald or skewbald like the one in the picture. Once a year in July they are rounded up and made to swim to the neighbouring island of Assateague.

[73]

The Quarter Horse [*left*] developed from a seventeenth century cross between Spanish and English horses. It was a popular horse for short races of about 440 yards, known as 'quarter milers', and the name has stuck. The English settlers missed going to race meetings and started their own informal sprint races between two horses on their land and even up the main streets of towns. They bred horses suitable which were compactly built and had well built shoulders and quarters to give them the power for a quick start and speed. The breed is very versatile and has remained popular for short races and all types of rodeo contests such as cutting, roping, barrel racing and bull-dogging. [*above*] A group of Quarter Horses on a stud farm. A Western Appaloosa wearing the distinctive saddle and bridle typical of the Western style of riding. The breast plate is designed to prevent the saddle from slipping. This 'armchair' cowboy saddle is big and heavy, but is perfectly comfortable for the horse if it is made of

good leather and fits well and is, of course, supremely comfortable for the rider, enabling him to spend all day in the saddle without tiring.

This riding style was originally brought to Mexico by the Spanish Conquistadores. Then it spread up into North America, where the American cowboys continued to ride in this manner. The basic difference from the classical style of riding lies in the reins being held in one hand, and the use of 'neck reining' to guide the horse. Classical riders may sometimes scorn western riding, but none the less it remains a very popular style amongst Americans.

The chestnut offspring of a palomino is basking in the sunshine unaware that his breeder had hoped he would share the gold and cream colouring of his mother. A palomino may happen by chance from any mating, no matter what the breed, but the highest percentage of successes is from palomino, chestnut and albino parents.

The Australian sun has scorched out
most of the goodness from the grass, but
these mares and foals have been well-fed
and cared for on a Victoria Stud [*right*].
Victoria is one of the richest Australian
states, and when its population quickly
multiplied with the discovery of gold,
the site of Melbourne was chosen as a
good place for a village. Now it is the
capital of course, and is the scene of the
Melbourne Cup, the country's most
important classic. Despite the inevitably
firm ground, some steeplechases are
included in programmes there.
Melbourne Cup day is like a state
holiday, when the racing fever takes hold
of people who take no interest in other
races, and thousands of enthusiasts flock
to the racecourse from all over the
country. The professional racing and
rodeo sports in Australia were very much
extensions of everyday life to the farmers
and horse owners in Australia because
horses were so widely used, and indeed
still are in certain areas and on the
larger stations. Bareback bronc riding as
a spectacle arose directly from the
traditional method of breaking in a
young horse [*left*] and informal races on
dirt tracks round the stations [*above*] test
the stamina of the horses as well as being
fun.

There are over 18,000 Aborigines in the Northern Territory and the government accepts them as full citizens and is trying to preserve their race and educate them. A great cattle industry thrives in the heart of Australia, the beasts living and growing on the drought-resistant grass and trees that cover the ancient plains. One man's herd might roam across a territory as large as some European states. [*above*] An Aboriginal stockman and [*left*] some of the cattle of the outback. The farmers use their horses to round up and count their cattle and to tend to their sheep, riding over land too rough for a car and going too far to walk. The farmer needs to inspect his boundary fencing and look for lost sheep in deep ravines. It is on some of the more remote stations in the hills of Western Australia that kangaroos can be seen. Some farms are run single-handed, or the farmer's sole helper is his wife and the only way they can take holidays is separately. Even if the stock is self-sufficient they never leave the farm for so much as a day because of the permanent worry of fire. Fire and drought are the biggest, most constant fears of these countrymen but nothing would induce them to live in the bustle of a town, for all its tempting security.

The rider [*right*] takes a well deserved drink. The temperature in the outback is often well into the hundreds, and both horse and rider must possess great endurance.

[79]

Every Easter the people of the countryside invade the city of Sydney. The Easter show of the Royal Agricultural Society of New South Wales is a worthy spectacle for the hundreds of thousands of visitors, and the Grand Parade [*above*] is a magnificent climax. Here the state's most valuable livestock, experienced handlers and accomplished horsemen parade in intricate patterns. The impressive display is the result of a masterpiece of organization. Throughout its duration the show provides a carnival, rodeo [*top left*], a stock sale, a shop-window and a fashion parade, besides, of course, giving entertainment with the horse and agricultural show classes

and exhibitions. It is a colourful, gay and lively affair worthy of the country's oldest state.

[*left*] A dramatic picture of local racing on dirt tracks. These stock horses are of indeterminate breeding, although on many stations the stock mares are covered by Thoroughbred stallions whenever they are available. The well-known Australian saddle horse, called the Waler after its state of origin, New South Wales, has now almost died out, and is no longer bred to the same standard as the horses which formed the bulk of the Australian cavalry division in 1914.

Racing Round the World

There have been one or two attempts to introduce trotting racing into England, mostly unsuccessful, but it is popular in Australia and America and also in Russia [*left*]. To some people trotting can seem a little like greyhound racing and more of a betting medium than anything else, but a great deal of skill is needed by the drivers to prevent collisions and overturning. Good horses are handicapped not by the amount of weight they have to carry, as in racing, but in the number of yards lead they have to give to their rivals at the start. And of course they must never break into a canter. [*above*] Women drivers pit their wits against each other in an American stadium.

Possibly the world's two most famous
racing scenes are Tattenham Corner
[*right*] and Becher's Brook [*left*], pictured
in 1972. The corner is raced around, and
the brook jumped over several times a
year, but it is the Epsom Derby and the
Grand National at Aintree, Liverpool
which have made them household names
throughout the world. Thousands of
people have just two bets a year, on
these two races. The Derby is the
greatest classic race for the best three-
year-olds in training, and the Grand
National is a race demanding such
luck, stamina, and jumping ability that
many of the best steeplechasers are not
even entered leaving the door to glory
open for lesser lights. Sadly the Grand
National has taken place under a
shadow of uncertainty concerning its
future in the last few years, because the
land may be sold for development, but
this has, if anything, increased its
popularity as an exciting spectacle.
The biggest upset in the Grand National
'lottery' in recent years was in 1967
when a loose horse ran across the
take-off side of the smallest fence on the
course, the one after Becher's Brook.
Chaos followed with loose horses and
riders everywhere, and those at the back
of the field could not even reach the
jump because there was such a muddle
in front of it. In the end it was *Foinavon*,
steered by Johnny Buckingham, who
found a gap right on the outside, and
was a fence clear before anyone else
could follow. His starting price was
100–1. Becher's Brook takes its name
from Captain Martin Becher, a top rider
and former soldier under Wellington,
who landed in the brook in the 1839
running of the Grand National. The

ence, four feet ten inches on take-off
side, has a drop so big that if a man
stands on the landing side, it towers
above him. The brook itself is five feet
six inches wide and if a horse takes off
too far back, or too close he is likely to
hit the lip of the ditch and come down.
To maintain balance on their mounts
jockeys slip their reins, lean back and
have their feet well forward. But having
taken it perfectly the chances are that a
jockey will find a fallen horse sprawled
across the landing side which may bring
him and his horse down. If a jockey
takes the fence on the inside he can cut
part of the corner, but the risk is greater
as the drop is steeper. Becher's is not the
biggest fence on the course. The massive
Chair in front of the stands is five feet
two inches high with a six feet wide ditch
on the take-off side.

The Derby draws bloodstock lovers from
all over the world to witness the finest
horseflesh in action. Tattenham Corner
is left-handed and has a strong influence
on the result of a race, many young flat
horses being unused to a sharp downhill
turn. In 1972 Lester Piggott, who will go
down as one of the greatest flat-race
jockeys of all time, won his sixth Derby
and twentieth English classic in all. He
was riding *Roberto* and just forced the
colt ahead of *Rheingold* ridden by Ernie
Johnson who, in his only previous ride
in the Derby in 1969 had won on
Blakeney. Piggott is not only master at
jockeyship, but has an uncanny way of
picking the right mount. In one Derby
in recent years he was the only jockey
in the race to have won it before; and
his position was unchanged at the end of
the race.

The British thoroughbred has led the racing world since its evolution over 250 years ago. On the occasions now when other countries rival British supremacy their horses largely stem from British blood. All thoroughbreds can be traced back to Arab stock on the male line; they originated from four stallions in the eighteenth century: the Darley Arabian, the Godolphin Arabian, the Byerley Turk and the Helmsley Turk. Racing as a sport is much older than the thoroughbred however; it was probably the Romans who introduced racing into Britain in the tenth century A.D. Racing has always been supported by the aristocracy, exclusively so in the early days. Queen Elizabeth I loved it and James I was keen; Oliver Cromwell opposed it politically and then later encouraged it, but it was under Charles II that racing really came into its own, and it is to his lavish spending that we owe the thoroughbred horse.

To own a racehorse is the ambition of many people from all walks of life (Gregory Peck's avowed ambition is to win the Grand National, and he has had a runner in it). This chestnut [*left*] is carrying the colours of Mr Paul Hamlyn. He is wearing blinkers to keep his mind on the job in hand, but this is not necessary for most horses who are bred for racing and quite simply love the sport.

The sacrosanct bastions of the Jockey Club were stormed in 1972 when, for the first time in the history of the British Turf, women were allowed to ride in twelve experimental ladies' flat races. Similar prejudice against lady jockeys in the United States was swept away a few years ago, after strong campaigning, particularly from Kathy Kusner. Before the end of the 1972 season in England it was announced that twenty ladies' races would be held in 1973, and a Lady Jockeys' Association has been formed. Miss Meriel Tufnell [*left*] became the first lady champion rider: she won the inaugural race at Kempton on her mother's *Scorched Earth* at a starting price of 50–1. His odds were much shorter when he again showed a clean pair of heels to his rivals in the second race, and Meriel gained a third victory at Newbury on Hard Slipper. With so few races, it was decided that the championship would be won by the lady who gained the most points by the end of the season. The runners in each race had to be decided by drawing names out

of a hat as there were always far too
many entries, and in the last race Meriel
did not have a ride. Before the race Mrs
Jennifer Barons was just one point
behind Meriel, who watched the race
from the stands with fingers clenched as
Mrs Barons brought her horse smoothly
into second place a furlong from home;
but then her horse suddenly faded, and
did not place, and Meriel emerged as
the champion lady rider.

The racing colours are similar to those
seen on the western race courses, the
jockey looks stylish, and there is an
impressive grandstand, but how on earth
will this horse see his way, and where is a
horse produced for a race with such a
magnificent mane [*right*]? The answer is
Warsaw, and the horse is an Arab. Arabs
are kept more for beauty and breeding
than for racing now, but Arab races are
still held in Warsaw and in some parts
of Russia, and the meetings, complete
with tote, are attended by enthusiastic
crowds.

All too often when a horse wins a top
class race as a three-year-old the owner
reaps the reward and puts him to stud
immediately rather than risk him being
beaten as a four-year-old. But in 1972,
English racing was blessed with two
sporting owners, two confident trainers
and, without doubt, the two very best
four-year-old racehorses. They were
Mr Paul Mellon's *Mill Reef*, trained by
Ian Balding, who had the 1971 Epsom
Derby and other victories to his credit,
and Mr and Mrs John Hislop's *Brigadier
Gerard*, unbeaten and with a victory over
Mill Reef in the 2,000 guineas in his
record. Their proposed meeting as four-
year-olds was understandably heralded
as The Race of the Century. Both horses
were unbeaten in their preliminary
races, which added fuel to the fire of
their competition. But its flame was
suddenly, unpredictably, tragically
extinguished. The racing world could
scarcely believe its ears; *Mill Reef* had
shattered a foreleg while on a normal
exercise canter at home. Now the race of
the century could never be run. Suffice,
perhaps, to call *Brigadier Gerard* the best
miler of his time, and *Mill Reef* the best
over one and a half miles. Right is the
Brigadier winning the Prince of Wales
Stakes at Royal Ascot on June 20, 1972,
ridden by Joe Mercer from *Steel Pulse*
(Geoff Lewis) and *Pembroke Castle* (A.
Murray) in convincing style.

It was in 1964 that *Arkle* [*left*] won his first of three consecutive Cheltenham Gold Cups; in 1966 that he broke his pedal bone at the pinnacle of his meteoric career, and in 1970 that he was put down. Yet he has become a legend and his very name conjures up all that is best in steeplechasing. To hear again a commentary of one of his races, to read about him, or simply to think about him fills one with nostalgia.

There are not enough words to do *Arkle* justice. He was a phenomenal steeplechaser. He never once fell in a race. He was seldom beaten and then usually by a horse carrying stones less weight than he was. Even on those few occasions he ran doggedly on until the finish. He possessed that special quality which no horseman can detect in advance and which is a combination of indomitable spirit and courage, a sense of competition and a love of life and of the work to be done. He was also a showman who loved the hero-worship from the crowds, and had a strong, recognizable character.

Throughout his remarkable career *Arkle* was blessed with a devoted trainer, Tom Dreaper, a devoted owner, Anne, Duchess of Westminster, and a devoted jockey, Pat Taffe. A race was named after him at Cheltenham, and he has been immortalized there by the skilful hands of Doris Lindor. Her sculpture, which is unmistakably *Arkle*, was commissioned by the Racegoers' Club. In addition she sculpted the *Arkle* models for the Royal Worcester Porcelain Company, and made the bronze of him for the Arkle Challenge Trophy.

Not all racing is with high-class thoroughbreds but whatever the standard a close finish is always exciting. Pintos, or painted horses, heroes of many a Wild West film, are seen [*right*] racing on dust in America. Many jockeys will wear goggles to prevent the dust getting into their eyes, and in Canada,

where the tracks can become mudbaths, the jockeys wear as many as six or seven pairs at a time, pulling the top pair down as it becomes too mud-bespattered to see through. At these, as at thorough-bred races there exists the friendly banter between owners over which animal is better, the money is laid with bookmakers or totalisator, a woman picks her fancy by its name or colours regardless of form and sometimes strikes lucky, the trainer discusses tactics with the jockey and, after the race is over, there are the inevitable post mortems on what happened.

Lester Piggott, who won his first Derby at the age of eighteen and a half on *Never Say Die*, comes from a family of top class steeplechase jockeys. He is probably the most experienced European jockey riding today and has ridden winners both abroad and in this country. He has won, in all, twenty classic races in Britain, including the Derby six times and the St Leger seven times, which is a record number of successes equalled only by Steve Donoghue and Jem Robinson. He has been Champion Jockey of Great Britain nine times.

In many countries of the world, riding as a leisure activity is very expensive. In others, horses still constitute the main means of transport and communication. On the left is a spectacular sight at the entrance to the Siq at Petra, Jordan. To reach this spot tourists leave Jerusalem at 4.30 am for the 206 mile journey skirting the Dead Sea. At the village of Wadi Musa cars are replaced by horses to take them to the Siq. This is a narrow passage between the fabulous pink cliffs which brings the riders out at the foot of the Nabataen Monastery. They walk for 45 minutes to reach the ruins where the view is superb, and then return the way they came.

[*above*] Another spectacular place with golden beaches, rocky coves, slender palms swaying gently beneath the Pacific sun; warm water lapping over a coral reef, lush vegetation, friendly people and attractive horses. This is Fiji, where the horses take visitors into the hilly interior, or along the shore and are fequently used instead of cars.

From one extreme to the other – the parting of ways [above] and superb co-operation and timing in unison [right]. In the bareback bronc competition at Cowboy Days Rodeo, Evanston, Wyoming, a rider and his horse make a perfect pattern in the air as the bronc triumphs. Rodeo is not only the most spectacular sport in the world, but it produces, by its very nature, the bravest, toughest and most skilful of riders. These daring men are the true descendants of the Wild West pioneers. A few men at the top of the sport earn themselves a good living but for many it is no more than a mixture of thrills and spills and little money. The cowboys learn from each other and share the luck of the draw in the horses they ride. For the bareback competition they have one hand on a handle attached to the girth, and they must stay on for eight seconds (two seconds less than for saddle bronc riding), and their free hand may not touch the horse. The cowboys know the horses well and the broncs all have their own particular characteristics. One or two horses acquire reputations for being quite unrideable even for the required eight seconds. The bronc riders become stars in the same way as do the champions in any sport.

[right] The girls take to the field for barrel racing. To turn round the end barrel having reached it at a flat-out gallop demands agility and swift response to the rider's commands from the horse, and balance from them both. Astute horses soon learn the game. Runs are timed and at the collegiate rodeo finals of USA in 1971 just nine-tenths of a second separated the first ten contestants in the short tun!

There was laughter and amusement all round at the 1972 Horse of the Year Show, Wembley, when three Shetland ponies won the obstacle driving contest [*left*]. They beat much bigger, faster horses by virtue of their nimbleness at turning corners.

The Horse of the Year Show is held in October and lasts for five days. There are a great many classes for hunters, hacks, show jumpers, heavy horses and ponies as well as the mounted games, the displays, the driving classes, the Quadrille, the personality show and the finals of the Prince Philip Cup. There is show jumping every evening and usually a different display from abroad each year; in 1972 the horses from the *Cadre Noir* gave a superb performance of dressage of the *Haute Ecole*. Television has made the events of the show well known to thousands of viewers and one of the more popular routines is when the heavy horses rake the arena in between each competition [*below*].

The Hackney class always provides a stylish reminder of the years before the car was invented, since the pony's proud bearing and high leg carriage make it a distinctive animal [*right*]. It is a tremendous trotter, and is now usually seen in harness although it began life as a Norfolk farm work horse. Almost every modern hackney is a descendant of the Darley Arabian, hence its stamina, speed, slightly dished nose, large eyes and small ears. The Norfolk trotter, as the hackney was first known, was bred about 1729. Not only was he a pack-horse on the farm, but he would carry both the farmer and his wife into market. One hackney in the early 1820s is said to have trotted twenty-four miles in an hour and another trotted two miles in five minutes four seconds, while *Nonpareil* was driven one hundred miles in nine hours fifty-six minutes and fifty-seven seconds. One of the most successful hackney breeders in Britain today is Mrs Ann Haydon, who shows horses herself in America and Canada as well as in Britain.

Although hunting has always been a popular sport amongst country folk, it is now attracting a large following amongst town people. This can create a problem in that ignorance of the country code angers farmers who may forbid a hunt to cross their land if they suspect their gates will be left open or that their crops will be damaged. This can be disastrous for a hunt at a time when available land is continually being eaten up by motorways and urbanization. Although some hunts are assured of a safe future through the long-standing patronage of a local landowner, several have been forced to amalgamate. Another factor to be reckoned with is the anti-blood sports league, whose members do their best to put fox hunting in a bad light. Few have hunted themselves, and most are ignorant of the fact that, although a sport, hunting is necessary to control foxes, which are vermin. The alternative methods are gassing, trapping and shooting. [*above*] The master of the Southdown hunt prepares to send the hounds in to draw a covert.

[*right*] A West Percy Huntsman waits for the hounds to find in very different country – the bleak moors of Northumberland where in fact there is excellent hunting since the valleys are well wooded and there are few problems of urbanization.

Left are two of Ireland's best known hunts, the Galway Blazers [*top*], and the Scarteen or Black and Tans [*below*], so-called because of their colouring. The dry-stone wall lining the lane is typically Irish. In this part of Ireland many of these walls are jumped in a day's hunting, as well as banks and ditches. Some look so wide and deep that many an inexperienced rider finds himself just holding onto the mane, shutting his eyes and praying! The challenging nature of the countryside, full of naturally high banks and hedges, makes the horses adept at tackling almost anything at speed. Ireland consequently produces the very best hunters, and attracts dealers and buyers from all over the world. There is a colourful tale behind the name, the Galway Blazers. In the early nineteenth century a Mr Robert Parsons Persse, Master of the Castleby Hunt, Galway, spent a riotous evening with friends at an inn in Birr. The festivities grew more and more uproarious and finally ended with the inn being burnt to the ground. The huntsmen have been known as the Galway Blazers ever since.

Fox hunting is one of the oldest English sports, and this meet [*right*] is set against the background of one of the oldest English castles, Alnwick castle in Northumberland. This is the family home of the Percys, Dukes of Northumberland, who first built their border stronghold in the twelfth century. The Duke of Northumberland is now Master of the Percy Hounds. The pack is pictured here with the huntsman, Don Claxton.

[*following page*] The huntsman of the Surrey Union Hunt encourages his hounds to work through thick plantation cover. It is a wooded area and this stocky, deep-chested heavyweight hunter is the ideal mount because the speed of a thoroughbred is not essential. His sturdiness enables him to negotiate sticky mud safely and he can hunt all day without overtiring. The huntsman's voice will be heard ringing through the woodland, and the field will wait expectantly on the far side of the covert, unable to see, but listening intently for the

first sound of tongue from a hound, picked up quickly by the whole pack. The fox will slip out from a far corner of the wood and if there is a rider sitting at that point he will quietly watch it leave and cross the field. When it has gone passed him he holloas. Riders pick up their reins expectantly, hoping the fox takes a good line for them to follow, and trusting their horses will jump well. The huntsman blows the 'Gone Away' on his horn, the pack is in full cry, and the chase is on. It may end half a mile away with a fall at the stile they had to jump to leave the wood. It may end with the scent gone dry, or it may end with a kill.

Pony trekking [*above*], is a fairly new pastime that has become a popular summer holiday occupation for children and adults, many of whom have never ridden before. There have been disturbing reports of trekking ponies being badly treated and of some centres taking advantage of the fact that many of their clients know little about horses, and so will not report under-nourishment, cruelty or even lameness. Fortunately, these centres are the exception but they effect the reputation of the majority who care for their ponies and employ conscientious staff. Trekking centres are found mostly where there is open land available for riding, such as Exmoor, Wales and Scotland. It gives people an opportunity to see beautiful, unspoilt tracts of land in the best possible way—on horseback—as well as to learn how to ride and look after their horses.

Left, the West Dulverton Point-to-Point. These local steeplechases are run by the hunt of the area and are occasions of absorbing interest to those who know the horses and riders involved and have watched them improving in the hunting field. Not all the several thousand visitors to a point-to-point will realize that there is more to the occasion than bookmakers and beer tents, or an annual day out with the children. Many of the horses running will have been hunting from November to February learning to gallop and jump and look after themselves in difficult conditions. Following this the point-to-point course is often the training ground for future National Hunt stars and some Grand National winners begin in this modest but invaluable way. Visitors to a point-to-point love the rural atmosphere and a sport which is in the best amateur tradition. The six minutes taken to gallop three miles and jump eighteen fences at about thirty mph is for many of the riders the culmination of months of hard training, which may end in disappointment; for others, it is just an exciting experience crowning a good season's hunting.

Mrs Mabel Forrest on Maeve [*above*], victor of the Ladies' Classic, the four-mile ladies' race at the Middleton point-to-point in Yorkshire.

Until 1972 the only races in which a woman could compete in Britain were ladies' races at point-to-points, their own hunt members' race, and the Newmarket Town Plate, a three and three-quarter mile flat race decreed by King Charles II

in 1695 and run in the morning on the second Thursday of October. There are also a few flat races for women but some of the most skilful horsewomen are to be seen in the ladies' races at point-to-points where their dash and determination is always popular with the crowd. It is often the fastest and most thrilling race of the day, as the horses are carrying a stone less weight than in similar men's events. All point-to-points must be run over three miles or more and are a good test of a horse's stamina, since he must be very fit to fight a close finish at the end of four miles.

Polo [*left*] was played in Persia and Assam at least five centuries BC and was very popular in India. Three members of the 10th Hussars based in India read an account of it one day, and having procured some sticks with crooked ends and a billiard ball, they went straight out to their chargers and began playing. As a result they were responsible for introducing the game to England in 1869. America started playing polo in 1883, and since then it has become an international sport. Polo is a very fast game and swift decisions have to be made. Consequently it has caught the imagination of the public, and especially so as popular public figures such as Prince Philip became involved with it. Between 1951 and 1959 his handicap rose to four, ranking him joint third in the country. He once played in fourteen matches in as many days, and although he was never seriously hurt, an injury to his wrist forced him to retire in 1971.

Index

Acknowledgments

The publishers would like to thank the following individuals and organizations for their kind permission to reproduce the pictures in this book:

Allen Bird, Appaloosa Horse Club — 32
Bavaria Verlag — 50, 55
Carnemolia, J. — 42 top, 76, 77, 78, 79, 80, 81
Colour Library International — 15, 26
Dailey, Arthur, Wolf, Wyoming — 33, 72, 73 top
Desjardins, M., Realites — 6, 7 bottom, 24 bottom
Fain, James, Logan, Utah — 75 top, 92, 93
Fox Photos — 84 top, 84 bottom, 85 top
Goldman, Luther C., — 73 bottom
Hamilton, William L., ZEFA — 19 bottom
Jung, K., ZEFA — 20
Keystone Press Agency — 41 bottom, 88 top
Lacey, E. D., — 35, 36, 37 top, 38 top, 40, 41 top, 42 bottom, 43, 85 bottom, 86 bottom, 89 centre and bottom, 94, 94 bottom, 103
Meads, J. — 96, 97, 98, 99, 102
Miller, Jane — 9, 10, 11, 14 centre, 14 bottom, 90, 91
Okapia, Frankfurt — 21, 24 top
Ostgathe, ZEFA — 7 top
Pfletschinger, H., Bavaria Verlag — 30 top
Ruthven, Ianthe, Michael Holford — 16 bottom
Spanish Riding School of Vienna — 51 top
Spectrum Colour Library — 8, 14 top, 17, 22, 25 bottom, 27, 37 bottom, 57 bottom, 58 top, 75 bottom, 100, 101
Spence, Margie — 68, 69
Sport and General Press Agency — 87 bottom
Thompson, Sally Anne — 1–4, 12, 13, 16 top, 18, 19 top, 23, 25 top, 28, 29, 30 bottom, 31, 38 bottom, 39, 44, 45, 46, 47, 48, 49, 51 bottom, 52 top, 52 bottom, 53, 54, 56, 57, 58 bottom, 59, 60, 67, 69, 70, 71, 74, 82, 83, 87 top, 88 bottom, 95
Walker, Don, Appaloosa Horse Club — 34
Wallis Photographer — 86 top